ECUADOR 2016 HUMAN RIGHTS REPORT

EXECUTIVE SUMMARY

Ecuador is a constitutional, multiparty republic with an elected president and unicameral legislature. In 2013 voters re-elected President Rafael Correa and chose members of the National Assembly in elections that were generally free and fair. In December 2015 the National Assembly approved 16 amendments to the constitution, including one that would eliminate term limits for the presidency and other elected positions, starting after the 2017 national elections.

Civilian authorities maintained effective control over the security forces.

The main human rights abuses were lack of independence in the judicial sector; restrictions on freedom of speech, press, assembly, and association; and corruption. Government regulatory bodies established under the 2013 communications law issued a series of sanctions, fines, and forced corrections and retractions, primarily against independent media and journalists. President Correa and his administration continued to engage in verbal and legal attacks against media and civil society. The government used presidential decrees to dissolve civil society organizations on broad and ambiguous grounds. Limits on freedom of assembly continued, particularly affecting environmental activists and indigenous groups protesting laws affecting their lands.

Other human rights problems continued: excessive force and isolated unlawful killings by security forces; arbitrary arrest and detention; and delays and denial of due process. Violence and discrimination against women, children, minority groups, and the lesbian, gay, bisexual, transgender, and intersex (LGBTI) community; trafficking in persons; and child labor persisted.

The government sometimes took steps to prosecute or punish officials in the security services and elsewhere in government who committed abuses, although in cases of public interest, political interference often resulted in impunity.

Section 1. Respect for the Integrity of the Person, Including Freedom from:

a. Arbitrary Deprivation of Life and other Unlawful or Politically Motivated Killings

There were no reports that the government or its agents committed arbitrary killings. Credible reports continued that security forces, particularly police units, used excessive force and committed isolated unlawful killings.

In November 2015 Francisco Cajigas, a Colombian citizen, was found dead, two weeks after the police detained him outside his house in Ibarra for allegedly breaking a car's mirror. After the autopsy and investigation process, Cajigas' family received his body with his cranium missing. On May 26, Vice Minister of Interior Diego Fuentes stated that an investigation was underway to determine possible police responsibility. In June the director of the Truth and Human Rights Commission of the Prosecutor's Office stated that an investigation was in progress due to allegations that Cajigas was a victim of an extrajudicial execution. According to local human rights activists, the prosecutor in charge failed to perform a thorough forensic examination at the start of the investigation. On October 10, the Attorney General's Office conducted a crime scene reconstruction.

A Quito-based human rights organization reported that an investigation continued into the death of John Jairo Urrutia Guaman, a 15-year-old who died in December 2015 while in police custody. As of December 7, the investigation remained in progress.

Human rights organizations reported additional alleged unlawful killings by security forces in Guayaquil and Carapungo, but no additional public information was available regarding law enforcement investigations.

b. Disappearance

There were no reports of politically motivated disappearances.

c. Torture and Other Cruel, Inhuman, or Degrading Treatment or Punishment

While the constitution and laws prohibit torture and similar forms of intimidation and punishment, some police officers reportedly tortured and abused suspects and prisoners, at times with impunity.

On May 31, approximately 80 police officers from the Maintenance of Order Unit (UMO) and Intervention and Rescue Group carried out an operation in the medium-security wing of the Turi Rehabilitation Center. Prisoners and human rights groups reported that UMO agents attacked prisoners with tear gas, batons, electric shocks, and kicks. On June 22, 13 prisoners filed a habeas corpus petition. On June 30, a judge in the Family, Woman, Children, and Adolescence judicial unit ruled in favor of the prisoners and ordered their transfer to another detention facility, respect for existing protocols and guarantees in all future operations carried out in the Turi center, and a public apology issued by the National Police. On July 25, the civil and commercial division of the court of Azuay nullified the process to adopt the habeas corpus petition, claiming the judge did not have the purview to rule on the petition. A second hearing on the habeas corpus petition took place on September 7. On September 28, a judge ruled that the inmates suffered cruel and degrading treatment. The judge ordered the inmates' transfer to other detention centers in the country, as well as medical and psychological care. The police officers involved in the operation were prohibited from entering any prison in the country. In addition, the judge ordered the Ministries of Justice and of Interior to offer a public apology and provide human rights training to prison authorities around the country on May 31, 2017, the first anniversary of the operation. Public Defender Ernesto Pazmino stated that the aggression against prisoners in Turi constituted "torture." Local human rights organizations, including the Ecumenical Human Rights Commission (CEDHU) and the Regional Human Rights Advisory Foundation, called on the government to improve human rights training for police officers and prison authorities.

Prison and Detention Center Conditions

Prison conditions were harsh due to food shortages, harassment by security guards against prisoners and visitors, physical abuse, and inadequate sanitary conditions and medical care.

<u>Physical Conditions</u>: While government authorities announced that the expanded prison capacity had reduced overcrowding, gross overcrowding continued in some prisons. On July 26, *El Universo* newspaper reported that 79 inmates from the Social Rehabilitation Center in Ibarra were transferred to a prison in Latacunga following a fire. According to the article, the Ibarra prison held 540 inmates, although its operating capacity was only 140 inmates.

Pretrial detainees and convicted prisoners were held together in some detention facilities. Despite the opening of new prisons with more modern amenities, prisoners and human rights activists complained about a lack of resources for inmates, which meant that prisoners or their families were expected to provide many basic supplies, including mattresses, clothing, toiletries, and medicines. In some facilities the health measures provided remained sufficient only for emergency care. Prisoners reported that medicines often were not available and that they had no access to dental care. Prisoners also complained of harsh living conditions, including sanitary problems, a lack of food, the poor nutritional quality of the food, and lack of heating and hot water. A human rights lawyer reported lack of access to potable water in certain prisons.

Reports continued that prison guards ordered female relatives of prisoners to remove their clothing prior to visits, and in some cases they subjected the relatives to inappropriate touching during security body searches. On June 28, government representatives told the UN Human Rights Committee that a protocol prohibits bodily searches and uses body scanners to search visitors.

Vulnerabilities in security remained a problem. Official information was unavailable concerning the national prevalence of deaths in prisons. According to local human rights organizations, prison authorities threatened family members of prisoners who died or suffered serious injuries to prevent them from making their complaints public.

On May 16, television station Teleamazonas reported that a fight between prisoners in the maximum-security wing of the Turi prison in Cuenca left one prisoner dead and seven injured.

Police conducted searches and raids in prisons throughout the year and discovered guns, grenades, ammunition, and drugs. They also continued to take action against criminal gangs operating within prisons, which sometimes involved prison authorities. On July 28, the newspaper *El Telegrafo* reported that law enforcement officials dismantled an extortion network operating in the Cotopaxi Social Rehabilitation Center. The network included a prison guard and an employee from a food services contractor. On November 24, *El Comercio* reported that a Guayas criminal court sentenced 10 individuals, including seven employees at a Guayaquil prison, to five years in prison for their role in allowing drugs and other prohibited items to enter the prison.

Administration: Despite improvements in recordkeeping in the new prison centers, upon completing their sentences some prisoners remained incarcerated due to bureaucratic inefficiencies, lack of recordkeeping on the length of their sentence or incarceration, and corruption. It was extremely difficult to obtain a firm release date from prison authorities, and the onus was often on inmates to schedule their own review boards.

Public defenders assisted inmates in filing complaints and other motions. Prisoners have the right to submit complaints to local and national human rights ombudsmen. Human rights activists stated that independent authorities did not sufficiently investigate allegations of poor prison conditions.

Justice Minister Ledy Zuniga reported that procedures existed for transferring prisoners to different locations outside of prison centers. Media, however, reported that in several provinces, police did not have enough official vehicles, and there were reports police officers used taxis to accompany prisoners to medical checkups and other outside visits.

Independent Monitoring: Independent nongovernmental monitors complained that their access to prisoners was limited. According to the Permanent Committee for the Defense of Human Rights (CDH), prison authorities placed strict limits on who can visit prisoners and monitor prison conditions, which led to a "progressive isolation of prisoners." Independent observers must submit in writing their reasons for visiting a prison, specifying general and specific objectives of the visit, as well as other information required by an administrative order. The CDH reported that many requests never received a response, which effectively prohibited independent monitors from accessing prisons.

Improvements: In newer prison facilities, prisoners may acquire goods through a biometric system, limiting the flow of cash currency among prisoners.

d. Arbitrary Arrest or Detention

The constitution and other laws prohibit arbitrary arrest and detention, but there were reports that national, provincial, and local authorities in some cases did not observe these provisions.

Role of the Police and Security Apparatus

The National Police maintain internal security and law enforcement. The military is responsible for external security but also has some domestic security responsibilities, including combating organized crime. Both the police and military are in charge of border enforcement. Migration officers are civilians and report to the Ministry of Interior. The National Police are under the authority of the Ministry of Interior, and the military is under the supervision of the Ministry of Defense. The National Police's internal affairs unit investigates killings by police and examines whether they were justified. The unit can refer cases to the courts.

An intelligence branch within the military has a role similar to the police internal affairs unit. The law states that the Public Prosecutor's Office must be involved in all investigations concerning human rights abuses, including unlawful killings and forced disappearance.

Corruption, insufficient training, poor supervision, and a lack of resources continued to impair the effectiveness of the National Police.

Civilian authorities maintained effective control over the police and the armed forces. The government has mechanisms to investigate and punish abuse and corruption, although some problems with impunity existed. According to official figures published on February 28, the National Police expelled 866 officials from its ranks between 2013 and 2016, including 83 during the first two months of the year. In late December 2015, media reported the arrests of 19 police officers involved in a corruption scheme that sold "passes" (workplace transfers) to other officers for $1,500 to $2,000 per pass (country's official currency is U.S. dollar). On May 30, *El Universo* newspaper reported that 27 former police officers were initially linked to the process. Four individuals were convicted, the prosecutors dropped charges against five individuals, and court proceedings continued against 17 other former police officers. On September 5, 15 police officers--including the former commandant of the National Police, Fausto Tamayo--and a civilian participated in a hearing held at the National Court of Justice. On October 31, the Provincial Criminal Court of Pichincha sentenced Tamayo and Lieutenant Alexis Cifuentes to 13 years and three months in prison for organized delinquency. On December 3, state-owned media outlet *El Telegrafo* reported that the Provincial Criminal Court of Pichincha sentenced nine defendants to nine years and three months in prison, while other individuals received sentences ranging from 10 months to five years.

Police receive required human rights instruction in basic training and in training academies for specialized units. In the police academy, human rights training is integrated throughout a cadet's four-year instruction. Additionally, there is a mandatory human rights training regimen concerning preservation of life and human rights, along with a human rights handbook. There were reports that police officers complained to local nonprofit groups about the lack of knowledge and preparation of police instructors teaching human rights in the academy. Authorities offered other human rights training intermittently. The government continued to improve the preparedness of police, including increasing funding, raising salaries, and purchasing equipment.

Arrest Procedures and Treatment of Detainees

The law requires authorities to issue specific written arrest orders prior to detention, and a judge must charge a suspect with a specific criminal offense within 24 hours of arrest. Authorities generally observed this time limit, although in some provinces initial detention was often considerably longer. Detainees have the right to be informed of the charges against them. By law, if the initial investigation report is incriminating, the judge, upon the prosecutor's request, may order pretrial detention.

Detainees have a constitutional right to an attorney. Indigents have the right to request a court-appointed attorney from the autonomous Public Defenders' Office. Although the number of available court-appointed defenders was higher than in previous years, the high number of cases and limited time they had to prepare for the defense of the detainees continued to represent a disadvantage during trials.

Although the law entitles detainees prompt access to lawyers and family members, human rights organizations continued to report delays depending on the circumstances and officials' willingness to enforce the law.

Pretrial Detention: Corruption; a lack of resources to train police, prosecutors, public defenders, and judges; and general judicial inefficiency caused trial delays. On June 28, a government delegation stated during its presentation to the UN Human Rights Committee that 30 percent of the 26,421 persons in detention had not received sentences.

Detainee's Ability to Challenge Lawfulness of Detention before a Court: Detained persons may challenge the legality of their detention through an appeal to any judge in the locality where the detention took place, and there is no time limit in which such an appeal must be filed. The detainee may also request bail or other alternatives (for example, house arrest or probation) to pretrial detention. Such alternatives are allowed only in cases of crimes punishable with prison terms of less than five years.

e. Denial of Fair Public Trial

While the constitution provides for an independent judiciary, outside pressure and corruption impaired the judicial process. Legal experts, bar associations, and human rights organizations reported on the susceptibility of the judiciary to bribes for favorable decisions and faster resolution of legal cases. Judges reached decisions based on media influence or political and economic pressures in cases where the government expressed interest. Delays often occurred in cases brought against the government, whereas cases brought by the government moved quickly through the courts. A nongovernmental organization (NGO), the judicial watchdog Observatorio de Derechos y Justicia, issued a report in June arguing that government officials implicated in a corruption scandal at state-owned company PetroEcuador received preferential treatment (see section 4), whereas persons critical of the government, including students and indigenous leaders, were subject to "disproportionate sanctions" for minor crimes or without evidence of any infraction. There were credible reports that the outcome of many trials appeared predetermined. According to human rights lawyers, the government also ordered judges to deny all "protectionary measures," i.e., legal motions that argued the government had violated an individual's constitutional rights to free movement, due process, and equal treatment before the law. Lawyers and human rights activists stated the government initiated disciplinary action based on "inexcusable error" against judges who allowed protectionary measures against the government.

Trial Procedures

The constitution and law provide for the right to a fair public trial, although delays occurred frequently. By law defendants are presumed innocent until proven guilty. Defendants have the right to be informed promptly and in detail of the charges.

The accused have the right to consult with an attorney or to have one provided, and to appeal. Defendants have the right to free interpretation as necessary from the moment charged through all appeals, but some defendants complained about the lack of an interpreter at court hearings. They have the right to adequate time and facilities to prepare defense, although in practice this was not always the case, and delays in providing translation services made this difficult for some foreign defendants. They also have the right to be present at their trial and to access evidence held by police or public prosecutors. The accused may also present evidence and call witnesses, invoke the right against self-incrimination, and confront and cross-examine witnesses. The law extends these rights to all defendants.

Judges reportedly rendered decisions more quickly or more slowly due to political pressure or, in some cases, the payment of bribes. There were reported delays of up to a year in scheduling some trials.

Criminal justice reforms aimed at reducing congested dockets in criminal cases produced "simplified" proceedings in pretrial stages, resulting in summary proceedings against defendants with few if any due process protections.

The regular court system tried most defendants, although some indigenous groups continued judge members independently for violations occurred in indigenous territory.

From June 6 to July 13, 121 Cuban citizens were deported because they did not have legal status in Ecuador. Authorities placed some Cuban citizens in a temporary detention center and a local jail prior to deporting them. Human rights lawyers argued the deportations violated the migrants' human rights because they did not receive due legal process. They also claimed that 40 Haitian citizens were deported without due legal process. Government authorities stated the migrants received due process in deportation hearings.

Political Prisoners and Detainees

There were no reports of political prisoners or detainees.

Civil Judicial Procedures and Remedies

Civil courts and the Administrative Conflicts Tribunal, generally considered independent and impartial, handle lawsuits seeking damages for, or immediate ending of, human rights violations. Civil lawsuits seeking damages for alleged wrongs by the government rarely were filed, since such suits were difficult to prosecute and time-consuming, with judges taking up to a decade to rule on the merits of a case.

Property Restitution

Human rights groups denounced forced evictions by government authorities without due process or timely relocation to other housing. The evictions mostly affected Afro-Ecuadorian families in urban areas or indigenous families living near natural resource extraction projects. According to human rights organizations, in some cases the government failed to provide timely restitution or compensation to evicted families.

f. Arbitrary or Unlawful Interference with Privacy, Family, Home, or Correspondence

The constitution and the law prohibit such actions, but there were reports the government failed to respect these prohibitions.

Human rights, environmental, and labor activists and opposition politicians reported physical surveillance by authorities, including monitoring of their private movements and homes. According to some human rights activists, the physical surveillance was an act of intimidation intended to silence any potential criticism of the government.

Section 2. Respect for Civil Liberties, Including:

a. Freedom of Speech and Press

The constitution provides for freedom of speech and press, but the government restricted these rights. The government continued to use the communications law to limit the independence of the press.

Freedom of Speech and Expression: Generally, individuals could discuss matters of general public interest publicly or privately without reprisal, although various civil society groups, journalists, and academics argued that the law limited their freedom of expression and restricted independent media. Under the 2013 communications law, media outlets are also legally responsible for the opinions of their contributors. Independent of this law, it is illegal for citizens to threaten or insult the president or executive branch, and penalties for violators range from six months to two years' imprisonment or a fine from $16 to $77.

Article 176 of the criminal code that went into effect in August 2015 establishes a prison sentence of up to three years for those who "disseminate, practice, or incite any distinction, restriction, or preference on grounds of nationality, ethnicity, place of birth, age, sex, gender identity or sexual orientation, cultural identity, marital status, language, religion, ideology, socioeconomic status, immigration status, disability, or health status with the aim of nullifying or impairing the recognition, enjoyment, or exercise of equal rights." According to some legal experts, the article could restrict freedom of speech.

Press and Media Freedoms: Freedom House continued to rate the country's press status as "not free." The domestic freedom of expression watchdog group Fundamedios reported 491 "attacks on freedom of expression" during the year, compared with 499 attacks in 2015. These included 168 sanctions of media outlets under the communications law; 94 cases of restrictions on digital rights, including censorship on the internet and cyber threats; and 88 cases of "abusive use of state power," including the withdrawal of official publicity, forced correction, cancellation of frequencies and programs, and arbitrary dismissals of employees. President Correa continued to criticize private media outlets and accused them of spreading lies and showing bias against his administration. During his October 22 national weekly address, Correa referred to private television station Teleamazonas as the "corrupt press," and he stated that he regretted his participation in a Teleamazonas news program on October 16. Regulatory bodies created under the 2013 communications law monitored and disciplined the media through a combination of legal and administrative sanctions.

Independent media remained active and expressed a wide variety of views, including those critical of the government, although many analysts and journalists noted the 2013 law had led to self-censorship in private media, pointing to a decrease in investigative reporting.

Provisions in the law limit the ability of media to provide election coverage during the official campaign period. A constitutional court ruling affirmed the right of the press to conduct interviews and file special reports on candidates and issues during the campaign period, but it left in place restrictions on "direct or indirect" promotion of candidates or specific political views.

The law includes the offense of inciting "financial panic" with a penalty of imprisonment for five to seven years for any person who divulges false information that causes alarm in the population and provokes massive withdrawals of deposits from a financial institution that places at risk the institution's stability. Some analysts viewed this as a warning to the media in their reporting on the country's financial problems. Media outlets reported privately that they refrained from some financial reporting due to concern over the possible legal consequences.

The government owned or operated an estimated 27 media outlets and used its extensive advertising budget to influence public debate. The law mandates the broadcast of messages and reports by the president and his cabinet free of charge. The government increasingly required media stations to broadcast statements by the president and other leaders, thereby reducing the stations' private paid programming. Various media outlets also reported pressure from the government to broadcast "voluntary" advertisements or face the risk of losing their broadcast frequencies. According to Fundamedios, many local and indigenous community radio stations stated that their contracts required them to broadcast the president's weekly address and send to Secom their daily programming list in advance.

The law calls for the redistribution of broadcast frequencies to divide media ownership between private media (33 percent), public media (33 percent), and community media (34 percent). Observers claimed this redistribution of frequencies would reduce the private media by almost 50 percent. The government asserted in public statements that information was a public service rather than a right and that the redistribution of frequencies guaranteed a more inclusive and diverse media environment. During the year the Agency for Regulation and Control of Telecommunications (Arcotel) and the Council of Regulation and Development of Information and Communication (Cordicom) initiated a process to adjudicate 1,472 radio and television frequencies. Media directors stated that the government had either directly or indirectly threatened revocation of their frequencies unless they limited critical coverage of the government. Fundamedios expressed concerns about a perceived lack of independence of Arcotel and Cordicom and a lack of citizen oversight. The NGO also noted that Arcotel planned to announce the results of the frequency competition in December, just a few months before the February 2017 elections, which Fundamedios argued would encourage self-censorship by media outlets. On July 11, Fundamedios called again for the suspension of the contest, noting that the number of applications for frequencies did not reach the number of available frequencies. On August 9, Fundamedios reported that Arcotel denied its request for information and the possibility of citizen oversight. On November 10, opposition legislator Lourdes Tiban called for the suspension of the frequency adjudication process due to allegations of corruption related to the adjudication of a frequency for a private media outlet in Manabi. During a December 2 hearing at the Inter-American Human Rights Commission, press freedom watchdog organizations stated that the frequency adjudication process suffered from a "lack of transparency" and other "irregularities."

<u>Violence and Harassment</u>: During public appearances and his weekly television and radio address, President Correa regularly questioned journalists' competence and professionalism and accused the private media of bias. He continued to cite individual journalists by name and encouraged both government officials and private individuals to raise complaints against the media. On September 15, Correa tweeted "cowards" in reference to journalists from the online news site *4Pelagatos*, following its publication of a column about Correa's daughter and an editorial she wrote for state-owned newspaper *El Telegrafo*. Other Twitter users published threats and the telephone numbers, addresses, and photographs of

4Pelagatos columnists Martin Pallares, Roberto Aguilar, Jose Hernandez, and Gabriel Gonzalez. NGOs, journalists, and international human rights organizations reported continued pressure from authorities against the media that resulted in threats against journalists and sanctions under the communications law. The Inter American Press Association reported that government-produced spots "discredit, harass, and persecute journalists, politicians, and media outlets."

On June 30, the Inter-American Platform of Human Rights, Democracy, and Development (PIDHDD) reported that unknown officials charged with enforcing the law temporarily detained journalist and human rights activist Mayra Caiza as she was taking photographs near the Turi detention center in Cuenca, as part of her investigation into the alleged torture against prisoners during a police operation on May 31. During her brief detention, the officials interrogated Caiza and deleted her photographs, including those not related to the Turi case. The PIDHDD requested further information about Caiza's detention from the interior and justice ministries and the Attorney General's Office. As of August 31, no further information was publicly available on any actions taken by the government.

On October 20, police stopped Ramiro Cueva, director of Ecotel TV, in Loja while he was in his vehicle. Video footage showed transit agents and police pushing Cueva to the ground and then a police officer placing his knee in Cueva's groin while Cueva lay on the ground. Transit agents stated that Cueva's vehicle was stopped because the vehicle's inspection was not up to date. According to Cueva, the deadline for the inspection was December 31, and his car's registration ran through 2019. Following the police operation, individuals at the scene placed Cueva in an ambulance so he could receive medical treatment. In December 2015 police and telecommunications regulators raided Ecotel TV and seized transmission equipment. According to Ecotel administrators, the government's actions were in response to Ecotel's late payment of a $151 licensing fee in 2002. The raid on Ecotel occurred just three days after President Correa attacked Cueva during a public address. Correa accused Cueva of lies and "politics masked as journalism" for an Ecotel report claiming that authorities covertly transported desks and furniture from one school to a new school the government inaugurated.

Censorship or Content Restrictions: Journalists working at private media companies reported instances of indirect censorship and stated that President Correa's attacks caused them to practice self-censorship.

The communications law requires the media to "cover and broadcast facts of public interest" and defines the failure to do so as a form of prior censorship. The superintendent of information and communications decides prior censorship cases and can impose fines. Many private media complained that the government could decide what is of "public interest" and thus unduly influence their independent reporting. After opposition politicians claimed that state-owned Ecuador TV's coverage of ruling party Alianza PAIS' political convention on October 1 violated election laws for an alleged use of public resources, Nadia Ruiz, acting director of RTV Ecuador Empresa Publica, stated that coverage of the convention was of "public interest." She noted that Ecuador TV did not transmit the conventions for two opposition movements because they "only confirmed the precandidates for the presidency." Oscar Bonilla, Alianza PAIS secretary of political action, claimed that covering the convention was "a responsible exercise of communication," but private media "sought to diminish" the event.

The communications law also imposes local content quotas on the media, including a requirement that a minimum of 60 percent of content on television and 50 percent of radio content be produced domestically. Additionally, the law requires that advertising be produced domestically and prohibits any advertising deemed to be sexist, racist, or discriminatory in nature. Furthermore, the Ministry of Public Health must approve all advertising for food or health products.

The government remained the largest single advertiser in the country. Media watchdog organizations argued that the government used advertising contracts to reward or punish media companies.

Private media outlets reported that the government continued to use tax and labor inspections to harass outlets that published reports critical of the government. These investigations forced the outlets to undertake time-consuming and costly legal defenses.

Libel/Slander Laws: The government used libel laws against media companies, journalists, and private individuals. Libel is a criminal offense under the law with penalties of up to three years in prison, plus fines. The law assigns responsibility to media owners, who are liable for opinion pieces or statements by reporters or others, including readers, using their media platforms.

On January 4, Judge Oswaldo Saritama Naula sentenced Loja municipal council member Jeannine del Cisne Cruz Vaca to 30 days in prison for discrediting the honor of Loja mayor Jose Bolivar Castillo. On September 21, Cruz had tweeted, "Mayor Jose Bolivar Castillo... all we ask…is that you stop lying and stealing."

On February 1, a criminal court in Loja ratified the 30-day prison sentence against Cruz.

On September 5, Quito vice mayor Eduardo del Pozo received a 15-day prison sentence for "discrediting the honor" of President Correa. According to Caupolican Ochoa, President Correa's lawyer, during a June 10 radio interview, Del Pozo had accused Correa of manipulating legal cases to obtain money, not paying taxes, and moving money to tax havens, which damaged Correa's honor and dignity. Del Pozo claimed the decision by Judge Maximo Ortega was "political persecution for thinking differently."

The law includes a prohibition of "media lynching," described as the "coordinated and repetitive dissemination of information, directly or by third parties through the media, intended to discredit a person or company or reduce its public credibility." The exact terms of this provision remained vaguely defined but threatened to limit the media's ability to conduct investigative reporting. The superintendent of information and communication has the authority to determine if a media outlet is guilty of media lynching and to apply administrative sanctions.

On August 8, the Superintendency of Information and Communications (Supercom) sanctioned television station Teleamazonas and journalist Janet Hinostroza on the basis of "media lynching" for distributing "damaging information to the prestige and credibility" of the National Public Procurement Service (SERCOP). The Supercom resolution indicated that two news programs released "concerted and repeated information on a reverse auction process of medicines, generating the perception that the process did not consider the quality of the pharmaceuticals" and did not allow for sufficient participation of SERCOP sources. Supercom ordered Teleamazonas to issue public apologies on the news programs, while Hinostroza received a written warning. The National Union of Journalists (UNP) criticized the Supercom decision as "another violation against freedom of expression." The UNP noted that the Supercom action occurred two days after President Correa called Teleamazonas' coverage "clear media lynching" during his August 6 national weekly address. In a subsequent interview with the Committee to Protect Journalists, Hinostroza stated that the ruling "demonstrates that in Ecuador it is not possible to do [investigative journalism]," adding that the communications law's intent is "to silence journalists that make [the government] uncomfortable."

Internet Freedom

The government did not restrict or disrupt access to the internet, but there were credible reports that the government censored online content and monitored private online communications without appropriate legal authority. A regulation requires that internet service providers comply with all information requests from the superintendent of telecommunications, allowing access to client addresses and information without a judicial order. Freedom House evaluated the internet as partly free. The International Telecommunication Union reported that 49 percent of the public used the internet in 2015.

While individuals and groups could generally engage in the expression of views via the internet, the government increasingly monitored Twitter and other social media accounts for perceived threats or alleged insults against the president and government officials. Some NGOs and media outlets reported cyberattacks by unknown perpetrators that appeared politically motivated, since they occurred during coverage of antigovernment protests and when content was perceived as critical of the government. On January 29, the Human Rights Foundation released a public statement condemning multiple distributed denial-of-service (DDoS) attacks on Fundamedios, days after the NGO launched a website that compiled alleged government attacks on independent media during 2015. On October 15, the Inter American Press Association reported that online portals *Focus Ecuador*, *Mil Hojas*, *Plan V*, and *4Pelagatos* suffered cyberattacks during the year.

Various local press outlets reported on the government's relationship with a Spanish antipiracy firm named Ares Rights that targeted internet websites, YouTube, and Twitter accounts critical of President Correa or of his government and forced these sites to take down content based on the Digital Millennium Copyrights Act (DMCA). The National Secretariat of Communication and Ares Rights sent DMCA takedown notices on behalf of several government officials, targeting documentaries, tweets, and search results that included images of those officials, alleging copyright infringement. On August 8, Fundamedios reported 806 complaints against 292 Twitter accounts between April 18 and July 21. According to Fundamedios, multiple complaints against certain Twitter accounts were directed at users who were critical of the government and had a high number of followers.

The law holds a media outlet responsible for online comments from readers if the outlet has not established mechanisms for commenters to register their personal data (including national identification card) or created a system to delete offensive comments. The law also prohibits the media from using information obtained from social media unless they can verify the author of the information.

Academic Freedom and Cultural Events

While there were no government restrictions on academic freedom or cultural events, academics reported that concerns over the process of awarding government contracts intimidated academics into practicing self-censorship.

b. Freedom of Peaceful Assembly and Association

Freedom of Assembly

The law provides for freedom of peaceful assembly. The government respected this right, with some exceptions. Public rallies required prior government permits that usually were granted. The government often deployed a large security presence at demonstrations. Security forces generally respected the rights of participants, but some exceptions occurred. On May 30, the criminal court in Loja sentenced Luisa Lozano and Servio Angamarca, members of the Saraguro indigenous nationality, to four years in prison for obstructing public services during a highway blockade in Loja Province in August 2015. According to the criminal code, obstructing public services is a crime punishable by one to three years in prison, but the judge added an additional year to their sentence due to "aggravating circumstances." The two persons were part of a group of 35 Saraguros that police detained during the blockade. Human rights organizations reported that police beat several Saraguros, including a pregnant woman, while clearing the blockade. The court absolved eight other defendants, while a case continued against a second group of 12 individuals. The defendants' lawyer claimed the conviction violated Lozano and Angamarca's constitutional rights, since an indigenous justice process had already declared the two individuals innocent on the premise that they were peacefully exercising their right to resistance. On October 20, the Criminal Sala of the Loja Court of Justice ratified the four-year prison sentence against Lozano and Angamarca. According to media reports and local human rights organizations, the court also sentenced three additional Saraguro members for obstructing public services, even though these members had been found not guilty by a lower court on May 30.

On May 31, Public Defender Ernesto Pazmino stated in a press release his concern about "disproportionate charges registered across the country." In subsequent media interviews, Pazmino called attention to the elevated sentences of the two Saraguro defendants. Pazmino proposed reforming the criminal code so that the blocking of public spaces during protests would no longer be subject to criminal penalties. In a July 7 interview with *El Universo*, Minister of Justice Ledy Zuniga accused Pazmino of lying due to political ambitions and urged him to resign.

A local human rights organization stated that police officers mistreated high school students during confrontations with the police that took place as part of an antigovernment protest on February 15-16. CEDHU and local media stated that police detained 20 students. A local newspaper reported that judges from the Judicial Unit of Young Offenders freed 14 minors on February 17 after sentencing each of them to pay a $50 fine and perform two hours of community service per week for three months. No public information was available on the judicial decisions for the six adult students.

Freedom of Association

The law provides for freedom of association, but the government took steps to limit this right. Presidential Decree 16, released in 2013, requires all social organizations (including NGOs) to reregister in a new online registration system within one year or face dissolution. In 2014 the National Secretariat for Policy Management announced that all NGOs registered in the old system would automatically be incorporated into the new system established under the decree. On June 29, the Ministry of Foreign Affairs stated that 77,160 social organizations were registered in the Unified System of Social Organizations. As of November, three challenges to the decree remained pending before the Constitutional Court.

In 2015 President Correa issued a decree to reform Decree 16. The changes, codified in Decree 739, eliminate a requirement that NGOs report their levels of foreign financing and removed their obligation to have assets worth at least $4,000 before registering as an NGO, while also placing foreign NGOs under the decree's regulations. Government officials argued that Decree 739 made it easier for NGOs to register, by eliminating the minimum equity requirement and standardizing the registration process so that the same requirements bind religious, community, and other organizations.

The decree provides the government discretion to dissolve organizations (including civil society, foundations, and churches) on multiple grounds, including compromising the interests of the government, engaging in partisan political activity, threatening public peace, deviating from the organization's stated purpose, or not providing access to information requested by the government. Provisions limit the ability of organizations to choose their members.

On July 20, the Ministry of Education initiated dissolution proceedings against the National Union of Educators (UNE), the largest teachers' union. UNE representatives stated the dissolution document did not cite specific wrongdoing but vaguely argued that UNE had violated the law and the union's charter (see section 7.a.).

On December 20, the Ministry of Environment initiated a process to dissolve environmental NGO Accion Ecologica, based upon a claim by the Ministry of Interior that the NGO had made social media posts that rejected mining activities in Morana Santiago Province and supported the "violent" acts committed by the Shuar protestors, that resulted in the death of a police officer at a mining camp on December 14. The government argued that the NGO had deviated from its stated purpose and negatively affected "internal state security" and "public peace" in violation of Presidential Decrees 16 and 739. As of December 31, the case against Accion Ecologica remained open.

c. Freedom of Religion

See the Department of State's *International Religious Freedom Report* at www.state.gov/religiousfreedomreport/.

d. Freedom of Movement, Internally Displaced Persons, Protection of Refugees, and Stateless Persons

The constitution and law provide for freedom of internal movement, foreign travel, emigration, and repatriation, and the government generally respected these rights.

Abuse of Migrants, Refugees, and Stateless Persons: Refugees, especially women and children, experienced sexual and gender-based violence. The Office of the UN High Commissioner for Refugees (UNHCR) and local NGOs reported that refugee women and children remained susceptible to violence and labor exploitation. They also reported the forced recruitment of adolescents on the northern border, particularly by organized criminal gangs that also operated in Colombia.

The government cooperated with UNHCR and other humanitarian organizations in providing protection and assistance to internally displaced persons, refugees, returning refugees, asylum seekers, stateless persons, or other persons of concern.

Internally Displaced Persons

Following an earthquake on April 16 that struck the Pacific coast, the government declared a "state of emergency" in the provinces of Esmeraldas, Guayas, Los Rios, Manabi, Santo Domingo, and Santa Elena. According to the final status report from the Secretariat of Risk Management on May 18, the earthquake claimed 663 lives and injured 6,274 persons. More than 40,000 persons were internally displaced following the earthquake, and approximately 29,000 were sheltered in public spaces, including sports stadiums. According to the International Organization for Migration, as of October 21, at least 12,000 persons remained in official and informal shelters.

Protection of Refugees

Access to Asylum: The law provides for the granting of asylum or refugee status, and the government has established a system for providing protection to refugees. The law establishes a two-step procedure for asylum seekers to apply for refugee status with a right to appeal rejections in the second stage of the process. The government limits applications for asylum to persons who enter the country within the previous 90 days. While an improvement over the previous 15-day time limit, experts noted that the admissibility procedure and a lack of qualified staff still hampered the granting of protection to deserving cases and remained the main challenges to refugee protection in the country.

The decree on refugee admissions establishes a timeframe of four months for the application process, but UNHCR and NGOs estimated the procedure lasted years in some instances. The decree establishes a timeframe of two months for decisions by the minister of foreign affairs and human mobility on administrative appeals, but decisions often took six months to a year. During the application process, an applicant receives an asylum-seeker card, renewable every two months, which grants the applicant the right to work until refugee status is adjudicated and all appeals are exhausted. A grant of refugee status is valid for two years but can be renewed.

Employment: Asylum seekers with family ties to Ecuadorian citizens can obtain a "dependent's visa," which offers permanent residence and full access to legal rights. UNCHR reported that a growing number of refugees renounced the refugee visa in order to obtain the dependent's visa.

Access to Basic Services: Forty percent of refugees and asylum seekers resided in isolated regions with limited basic services, primarily along the northern border, or in poor urban areas of major cities such as Quito and Guayaquil. According to

UNHCR and NGOs providing social services to refugees, refugees continued to encounter widespread discrimination in employment and housing. On September 15, UNHCR and the Civil Registry signed an agreement that would enable recognized refugees to receive national identification cards that facilitate their access to education, employment, banking, and other public services.

Durable Solutions: Societal stereotypes and media reports portraying refugees as criminals and prostitutes affected refugees' ability to assimilate into the local population. Few refugees were able to naturalize as citizens or gain permanent resident status, due to the expensive and lengthy legal process required. The main durable solution remained local integration, even though there were many obstacles to achieve sustainable local integration.

Temporary Protection: While there is no legal provision for temporary protection, the government and NGOs provided humanitarian aid and additional services, such as legal, health, education, and psychological assistance, to refugees recorded as having crossed the border during the year. Most government assistance ended after denial of official refugee status.

As an associate member of Mercosur, Ecuador issues the Mercosur temporary visa to citizens of the countries parties to or associated with the trade bloc. The agreement covers citizens of Argentina, Bolivia, Brazil, Chile, Colombia, Paraguay, Peru, and Uruguay, and the government waived the visa application fee (normally $230) for Colombian and Paraguayan citizens. Foreigners in an irregular migratory status in the country were eligible to apply for the visa. While the Mercosur visa does not provide any safeguard against forced repatriation, UNHCR noted that many persons opted for the visa, since it is faster than the refugee process and carries less social stigma. Visa recipients are able to work and study for a period of two years. The visa is renewable, but the requisites for such renewal were unclear to refugee advocates.

Section 3. Freedom to Participate in the Political Process

The law provides citizens the ability to choose their government in free and fair periodic elections held by secret ballot and based on universal and equal suffrage. In December 2015 the National Assembly approved a constitutional amendment to eliminate term limits for all elected positions, including the president, starting after the 2017 national elections.

Elections and Political Participation

<u>Recent Elections</u>: In 2013 the government held elections for national offices, including the presidency and the multiparty National Assembly. The Organization of American States (OAS), Inter-American Union of Electoral Organisms, Union of South American Nations, and domestic observers judged the elections open, free, and well organized, despite some recurring and limited local irregularities. Although the international and domestic observation teams reported no major fraud, some reports of missing or marked ballots and of counting and vote-tabulation irregularities resulted in challenges filed with the National Electoral Council (CNE) and Electoral Contentious Court (TCE), the appeals body for electoral matters. Opposition candidates claimed the CNE and TCE did not address irregularities transparently. The OAS reported the precampaign period featured "differential access and exposure of the contenders in the media." Furthermore, during the campaign period, there was unequal coverage of parties and candidates in news reports, depending on the ownership of the media. According to media monitoring by the local NGO Participacion Ciudadana, President Correa and his political supporters had a significantly greater presence in both public and private media than other candidates.

<u>Political Parties and Political Participation</u>: Electoral laws require political parties to register with the CNE. In order to receive authorization to participate in elections, parties and movements need to show the support of at least 1.5 percent of the electoral rolls by collecting voters' signatures. The law requires registered parties to obtain minimum levels of voter support to maintain registration. Voters are restricted to registering with only one political group.

On September 26, the CNE signed an agreement with Participacion Ciudadana that would enable the civil society organization to conduct a "quick count" of the February 2017 national elections.

Opposition alternate legislator Henry Llanes presented a complaint against President Correa, Vice President Glas, and several state-owned media outlets over alleged electoral infractions related to the live transmission of Alianza PAIS' political convention on October 1. On November 11, TCE judge Patricia Zambrano ruled against Llanes' complaint. Zambrano subsequently tweeted a message of gratitude to Alianza Pais (AP) supporters who accompanied the ruling party's presidential and vice presidential candidates' registration at the CNE on November 16. Following complaints that Zambrano's tweet demonstrated political partisanship, the TCE accepted Zambrano's resignation on November 24.

On November 11, Fernando Villavicencio registered his candidacy for a National Assembly seat in the province of Pichincha with the CREO (Creating Opportunities) opposition party. On November 14, Gustavo Baroja, prefect of Pichincha and provincial leader of ruling party AP, objected to Villavicencio's candidacy, noting that electoral law requires a candidate to resign from any political party 90 days before registering as a candidate for a separate party, unless the candidate receives authorization from the party to which he belongs. On November 17, the CNE accepted Baroja's objection, based on Baroja's argument that Villavicencio was affiliated with the Pachakutik party. On November 21, Villavicencio appealed the decision to the TCE, arguing that a document dated November 10 from Pachakutik's coordinator authorized him to register as a candidate for CREO. Villavicencio also claimed that the decision to bar him from running was politically motivated, citing his public denunciations of corruption in state-owned oil company PetroEcuador. As of November 25, the TCE had not issued a ruling. In 2013 Villavicencio received an 18-month prison sentence for defamation of President Correa, although Villavicencio went into hiding and the sentence was subsequently reduced to 12 months and then vacated. As of late November, legal proceedings continued against Villavicencio over his alleged publication of private emails from senior government officials.

<u>Participation of Women and Minorities</u>: The constitution provides for government-promoted, gender-balanced representation in the public sector, including in the lists of political parties' candidates for the National Assembly and other representative institutions. The electoral law mandates that electoral lists be gender balanced and structured in an alternating male-female (or vice versa) pattern for both primary and alternative candidates.

As of late September, the president's cabinet included eight women out of 36 ministers and national secretaries. The National Assembly featured 59 women among the 137 legislators, including three women in the principal leadership positions. In the February 2014 local elections, two of the 23 elected prefects were women. According to a report by *El Comercio*, three women were elected mayors in a sample of 30 provincial capitals and other large cities.

Minorities were underrepresented in political positions at the local and national levels in proportion to their representation in the overall population.

Section 4. Corruption and Lack of Transparency in Government

The law provides criminal penalties for corruption by officials. The government did not implement the law effectively, and officials often engaged in corrupt practices with impunity. The government took some steps to address official corruption. It continued a process to reform the judiciary, which improved the judiciary's ability to remove corrupt or ineffective judges. Many civil society activists noted, however, that judges on the higher courts appeared more closely aligned with the current administration, and many questioned the independence of those courts, especially in politicized cases. Media reports alleged police corruption and corruption in public contracts and procurement, including in state-owned companies. Labor leaders and business owners reported corruption among labor inspectors.

Corruption: On May 16, police arrested Alex Bravo, the manager of public oil company PetroEcuador, for influence peddling. On August 10, the Attorney General's Office modified Bravo's charges by including the charge of illicit enrichment; later, charges were further expanded to include acceptance of bribes from the company Oil Services & Solutions. On October 5, Alexis Mera, President Correa's legal secretary, announced that Bravo received $12 million in bribes and kickbacks during his tenure at PetroEcuador. The Attorney General's Office charged 17 individuals, including Bravo, former minister of hydrocarbons Carlos Pareja, and their relatives in connection with the PetroEcuador corruption case. A Quito criminal court held a preliminary hearing to review evidence on October 21. The judge ordered pretrial detention for nine suspects and prohibited the other suspects from departing the country. According to media reports, 14 of the 17 suspects, including former minister Pareja, had already fled the country. On October 23, the justice and interior ministers announced that the government had requested that Interpol issue "Red Notices" for eight suspects outside of Ecuador. On November 23, prosecutors added charges of illicit enrichment against Pareja, Bravo, and other defendants. On December 2, *El Comercio* reported that criminal investigations related to money laundering, illicit enrichment, bribery, and organized crime remained in process against 80 individuals, with six under arrest and 24 facing criminal charges. As of December the case remained in progress.

On December 21, unnamed Ecuadorian officials were cited among those taking bribes from the Brazilian construction and engineering company Odebrecht. Odebrecht admitted to making more than $33.5 million in corrupt payments to government officials in Ecuador between 2007 and 2016. The company realized benefits of more than $116 million as a result. As of December 31 an investigation into corruption claims related to public works projects managed by Odebrecht remained in progress.

There were other reported instances of corruption involving lower-level government officials, judges, and police officers. In April the Center for the Study of Bribery and Extortion Situations issued a report that described several cases of extortion experienced by rural women, including monetary demands from police officers and sexual and monetary demands from government officials in rural parishes.

Financial Disclosure: Government officials are required to declare their financial holdings upon taking office and if requested during an investigation. All agencies must disclose salary information annually. The constitution requires civil servants to present a sworn statement regarding their net worth at the beginning and end of their term of office, including their assets and liabilities, as well as an authorization to lift the confidentiality of their bank accounts. All declarations are filed in the offices of public notaries and are entered as a public document. The comptroller general's website contains a section where the public can conduct a search on officials to see if the officials complied with the income and asset disclosure requirement. There are no criminal or administrative sanctions for noncompliance, except for the inability to assume office. Public officials are not required to submit periodic reports, even when changes occur in their holdings.

Following the May 2015 arrests of a National Assembly member and two other public officials on corruption charges, National Assembly president Gabriela Rivadeneira requested that the comptroller general investigate the declared assets of all 137 lawmakers. In May 2016 media reported that six legislators remained under investigation due to possible evidence of criminal liability. As of November 1, the Office of the Comptroller General had not made public the results of the investigation.

Public Access to Information: The constitution and other regulations provide for the right of public access to government information, but authorities did not effectively implement the law. The law requires all public and private organizations that receive public funds to respond to written requests for information, publish specific information on their website, and submit an annual report to the Ombudsman's Office that details their compliance with the transparency law. Because of this legislation, government agencies increasingly included budget information, functions, organizational information, lists of government officers, and official notices on the internet in addition to responding to written requests. Nevertheless, the government did not always grant requests for information, and the government made exceptions, stating that the requested information was not available. Judges did not enforce the legislation requiring the government to release information.

Opposition legislators complained that although the law allows them to request information directly from government institutions, President Correa instructed government ministers to respond only to requests for information channeled through the president of the National Assembly.

Section 5. Governmental Attitude Regarding International and Nongovernmental Investigation of Alleged Violations of Human Rights

A number of domestic and international human rights groups generally operated without government restriction, investigating and publishing their findings on human rights cases. Government officials were somewhat cooperative and responsive to their views.

Civil society organizations expressed concern about the government's discretion to dissolve NGOs per Decrees 16 and 739 (see section 2.b., Freedom of Association). Decree 16 created the National Secretariat of Policy Management, an authority responsible for regulating the fulfillment of the objectives and activities of social and civic organizations. Civil society representatives argued that the vague and overly broad grounds for dissolution led to self-censorship among NGOs. Additionally, NGOs contended that challenging an order of dissolution via the judicial process might take several years.

International NGOs are also subject to the NGO regulations in Decree 739. The government continued to claim many NGOs were tools of foreign governments that destabilize the government.

The government criticized the credibility of specific international and local NGOs and their findings during public appearances, including the president's weekly television and radio address.

The United Nations or Other International Bodies: The government continued to lead an effort to disparage and weaken the Inter-American Human Rights Commission (IACHR) and often refused to send representatives to the IACHR's public hearings. The government refused to allow the IACHR to visit to investigate human rights problems in the country. On October 10, President Correa called for a new Inter-American System of Human Rights, arguing that the IACHR is an expression of "neocolonialism."

<u>Government Human Rights Bodies</u>: The Ombudsman's Office, which the constitution describes as an administratively and financially independent body under the Transparency and Social Control Branch of government, focused on human rights problems. The Ombudsman's Office regularly presented cases to the Public Prosecutor's Office.

A special unit within the Prosecutor's Office has responsibility for investigating crimes revealed in the 2010 Truth Commission report on alleged human rights abuses that occurred between 1984 and 2008.

Section 6. Discrimination, Societal Abuses, and Trafficking in Persons

Women

<u>Rape and Domestic Violence</u>: The law criminalizes rape, including spousal rape and domestic violence. Rape is punishable with penalties of up to 22 years in prison. The criminal code includes spousal rape under crimes against sexual and reproductive integrity. The penalty for rape where death occurred is from 22 to 26 years' imprisonment.

A 2011 government study found that 60 percent of women suffered from gender-based violence at some point during their lifetimes. Rates of abuse were highest among indigenous and Afro-Ecuadorian communities. On August 15, citing figures from the Coordinating Ministry of Security, *El Comercio* newspaper stated that 2,368 sexual attacks were reported between January and July, compared with 2,803 attacks during the same period in 2015.

According to local experts, reporting rapes and other forms of violence continued to be a traumatic process, particularly for female minors. For example, a rape victim must file a complaint at the Public Prosecutor's Office, and the victim must submit to gynecological evaluations akin to rape kits administered by medical experts. Many individuals did not report cases of rape and sexual assault because of the victims' fear of retribution from the perpetrator or social stigma.

Domestic violence is punishable with penalties ranging from four days to seven years in prison. The law provides penalties for physical violence, psychological violence, and sexual violence. According to the law, a prosecutor must investigate the victim's complaint of domestic abuse before issuing a restraining order. There were reports that in some cases victims waited 10 days or more for a response from the Prosecutor's Office. According to the law, domestic violence may be punished with a fine for "damages, pain, and suffering" ranging from $350 to $5,300, depending on the severity of the crime. The law also gives family courts the power to remove an abusive spouse from the home if continued cohabitation creates a risk to the victim of abuse. The law requires public hospitals to provide "first reception halls" to handle cases of sexual violence and domestic violence. The specialized halls--under the supervision of the Ministry of Health and staffed by physicians, psychologists, and social workers--offer immediate attention to the victim. The Ministry of Social and Economic Inclusion, together with some local and provincial governments and NGOs, also provides psychosocial services to victims of sexual and domestic violence. The ministry subsidizes shelters and other initiatives, including medical services at care centers and private clinics. The ministry does not publish public data on the number of shelters it funds, which were primarily located in the largest cities. According to NGO Fundacion Maria Amor, as of March there were five shelters nationwide for women who had suffered violence. Several women's rights organizations stated that the government did not have the resources to support victims of sexual and domestic violence. Fundacion Maria Guare reported that the city of Guayaquil, with a population of more than three million, had only one shelter for abused women and children, with a capacity for 40 persons.

Based on 2016 statistics, there were 50 judicial units and 78 courts specializing in gender-based violence. The judicial units have responsibility for collecting complaints and assisting victims may order arrest warrants for up to 30 days of detention against the aggressor. The units forward serious abuse cases to prosecutors for criminal prosecution. Human rights activists stated that 16,000 cases of domestic violence were pending in the court system. They argued that the court system was not sufficiently staffed to deal with the caseload and that judges lacked specialized training for dealing with gender-based violence.

Sexual Harassment: The criminal code criminalizes sexual harassment and provides penalties of three to five years in prison. Despite the legal prohibition of sexual harassment, women's rights organizations described harassment in public spaces as common. There were reports of sexual harassment on public transportation.

Reproductive Rights: The law acknowledges the basic right of couples and individuals to decide the number, spacing, and timing of their children; manage their reproductive health; and have the information and means to do so, free from discrimination, coercion, or violence. Some women's rights activists complained of the lack of formal sexual education, the ineffective distribution of birth control, and the social stigma that discouraged women from seeking family planning services.

<u>Discrimination</u>: The constitution affords women the same legal status and rights as men. The law also provides that the government should formulate and implement policies to achieve gender equality, incorporate a gender focus into plans and programs, and provide technical assistance to implement the law in the public sector. Nevertheless, discrimination against women was prevalent, particularly with respect to economic opportunities for older women and for those in the lower economic strata. According to a government study published in March 2015, women's average monthly income was $444, compared with men's average monthly income of $548.

Children

<u>Birth Registration</u>: Citizenship is acquired through birth in the country, birth to an Ecuadorian mother or father abroad, or by naturalization. In 2013 a study by the vice presidency revealed that 5.5 percent of the population were not registered at birth. According to 2014 statistics, ethnic minority families with limited economic resources continued to show registration rates significantly lower than those of other groups. Government brigades traveled to remote rural areas to register families and persons with disabilities. While the law prohibits schools from requesting civil registration documents for children to enroll, some schools, mostly public schools, continued to require them. Human rights organizations reported that the problem particularly affected refugee children. Other government services, including welfare payments and free primary health care, require some form of identification.

<u>Education</u>: According to the constitution, education is obligatory through ninth grade and free through 12th grade. Nonetheless, costs for school-related items, such as uniforms and books, as well as a lack of space in public schools, continued to prevent many adolescents from attending school. In some provinces children were assigned to schools outside their neighborhood, and school buses were not made available.

<u>Child Abuse</u>: According to 2015 figures from the Office of the Public Prosecutor, family members of the victim perpetrated the sexual abuse in 98 percent of the cases. Police estimated that more than 40 percent of child abuse cases were not reported to authorities. According to media reports, one in four children suffered

sexual violence in 2013. A 2013 study by Plan International found that 69 percent of children between the ages of 10 and 15 were victims of violence. NGOs reported that children living in the streets or in rural parts of the country, many from poor indigenous families, suffered from exploitative conditions.

Bullying remained a problem in schools and increasingly occurred on social media.

Early and Forced Marriage: The legal age of marriage is 18. In June 2015 a procedural code went into effect that repeals provisions that had allowed marriage before the age of 18, with the exception that legally emancipated minors can marry at age 16.

Sexual Exploitation of Children: The law prohibits sexual exploitation of children, including child pornography, with penalties of 22 to 26 years' imprisonment. The age of consent is 14. The penalty for commercial sexual exploitation of children under the age of 18 is 13 to 16 years in prison. Commercial sexual exploitation of minors remained a problem, despite government enforcement efforts.

International Child Abductions: The country is a party to the 1980 Hague Convention on the Civil Aspects of International Child Abduction. See the Department of State's *Annual Report on International Parental Child Abduction* at travel.state.gov/content/childabduction/en/legal/compliance.html.

Anti-Semitism

There was a small Jewish community, including an estimated 250 families in Quito and 120 families in Guayaquil, according to local synagogues. Isolated instances of anti-Semitism occurred. In September the Ministry of Justice, Human Rights, and Worship sanctioned the director and chief of security of the Quito Provisional Detention Center for allowing the use of an official stamp with a Nazi swastika for visitors entering the facility. The ministry condemned the use of any offensive symbol that could compromise one's human rights.

Trafficking in Persons

See the Department of State's *Trafficking in Persons Report* at www.state.gov/j/tip/rls/tiprpt/.

Persons with Disabilities

The law prohibits discrimination against persons with physical, sensory, intellectual, and mental disabilities in employment, education, air travel and other transportation, access to health care, or the provision of other government services. The National Council on Disability Equality oversees government policies regarding persons with disabilities. Although the law mandates access to buildings and promotes equal access to health, education, social security, employment, transport, and communications for persons with disabilities, the government did not fully enforce it. The law requires that 4 percent of employees in all public and private enterprises with more than 25 employees be persons with disabilities.

The law grants persons with disabilities the right to cost and fee reductions from several public and private entities, including utilities, transportation, and taxes. It also stipulates rights to health facilities and insurance coverage, increases access and inclusion in education, and creates a new program for scholarships and student loans for persons with disabilities. In 2015 the government-owned newspaper *El Telegrafo* cited a study by the Technical Secretariat for the Inclusive Management of Disabilities that 65 percent of persons with disabilities finished primary education and 7 percent pursued university studies. The law provides for special job security for those with disabilities or those who care for a person with disabilities, and it entitles employees who acquire a disability to rehabilitation and relocation. A national system evaluates and registers persons with disabilities. Many of the benefits in the law are transferable to a parent or primary caregiver. The law also gives the Office of the Human Rights Ombudsman responsibility for following up on alleged violations of the rights of persons with disabilities and stipulates a series of fines and punishments for lack of compliance with the law.

Advocates for persons with disabilities reported procedural regulations that went into effect in 2013 reduced coverage, protection, and the legal recognition of some persons with disabilities. For example, individuals with disabilities considered less inhibitive--those that restrict their capacity to perform less than 40 percent of essential everyday activities--lost access to certain economic benefits, including subsidized health care, home loans, special retirement and disability payments, and reduced fees in utility services. Advocates for persons with disabilities noted that the regulations contradicted labor laws, which require companies with at least 25 employees to hire persons with disabilities that restricted their capacity to perform less than 30 percent of essential everyday activities. Citing official figures, they argued that the 2013 regulations could affect access to economic benefits for up to 98,000 persons with disabilities of between 30 and 39 percent.

The government continued a campaign to create jobs for persons with disabilities, provide funding to municipalities to improve access to public buildings, and open training and rehabilitation centers. The initiative also monitored the degree of compliance by companies that hire persons with disabilities. The caregivers of persons with more significant disabilities received a monthly government subsidy of $240. The Technical Secretariat for Disabilities reported that between 2010 and 2014, there were 353,000 persons with disabilities registered, and 73,500 were incorporated into the labor market. According to a government study, the poverty rate for persons with disabilities fell from 42 percent in 2006 to 28 percent during the year.

The law directs the electoral authorities to provide access to voting and to facilitate voting for persons with disabilities, and international observers commended the government's accommodations for persons with disabilities in the 2014 local elections. The CNE initiated a program to allow in-home voting for those with more significant disabilities.

National/Racial/Ethnic Minorities

The constitution declares the state to be plurinational and affirms the principle of nondiscrimination by recognizing the rights of indigenous, Afro-Ecuadorian, and Montubio (an independent ethnic group of persons with a mixture of Afro-Ecuadorian, indigenous, and Spanish ancestry) communities. It also mandates affirmative action policies to provide for the representation of minorities. In 2009 the government began implementing a national plan to eradicate racial discrimination and exclusion based on ethnic and cultural differences.

Afro-Ecuadorian citizens, who accounted for approximately 7 percent of the population according to the 2010 census, suffered pervasive discrimination, particularly with regard to educational and economic opportunity. Afro-Ecuadorian organizations noted that, despite the absence of official discrimination, societal discrimination and stereotyping in media continued to result in barriers to employment, education, and housing. Afro-Ecuadorians continued to assert that police stopped them for document checks more frequently than they stopped other citizens.

Indigenous People

The constitution strengthens the rights of indigenous persons and recognizes Kichwa and Shuar as "official languages of intercultural relations." The law provides indigenous persons the same civil and political rights as other citizens. The constitution grants indigenous persons and communities the right to prior consultation before the execution of projects that affect their rights. It also provides for their right to participate in decisions about the exploitation of nonrenewable resources located on their lands and that could affect their culture or environment. The constitution also allows indigenous persons to participate in the economic benefits that natural resource extraction projects may bring and to receive compensation for any damages that result.

In the case of environmental damage, the law mandates immediate corrective government action and full restitution from the responsible company, although some indigenous organizations asserted a lack of consultation and remedial action. The law recognizes the rights of indigenous communities to hold property communally, although the titling process remained incomplete in parts of the country.

Indigenous groups continued to challenge government decisions and laws covering mining, water resources, and hydrocarbon resources that did not consider indigenous viewpoints, their right to prior consultation, or intruded upon indigenous autonomy over their lands and resources. On July 11, the UN Human Rights Committee expressed concerns over reports that the government granted natural resource concessions in indigenous territories without prior consultation and the potential negative impact of natural resource exploitation projects on indigenous peoples in voluntary isolation.

On August 11, the criminal court of Morona Santiago sentenced indigenous leader Tomas Jimpikit, president of the Shuar Bomboiza Association, to one year in prison for paralyzing public services during a social protest on August 14, 2015. Five other individuals were found not guilty. On that same day, human rights organizations and the Confederation of Indigenous Nationalities of Ecuador (CONAIE) reported that police and military forcibly evicted residents of indigenous community Shuar Nankints, in the province of Morona Santiago, in relation to a mining project. On November 21, Minister of Interior Diego Fuentes reported that Shuar members attacked a Chinese-owned mining camp in the southern Amazon region of Morona Santiago. Fuentes announced that charges of attempted murder would be brought against those involved in the attack. President Correa denounced the violence and stated that 14 police officers were injured, one critically. CONAIE and CEDHU called on the interior and defense ministries to halt incursions by security forces into Shuar communities to avoid further bloodshed. The Ministry of Defense rejected allegations by CONAIE that soldiers attacked the Shuar Nankints community and killed two Shuar.

On December 14, Coordinating Minister of Security Cesar Navas announced a 30-day state of emergency in the Amazon province of Morona Santiago, declaring that a police officer died during an attack by "illegal armed groups." On December 14, members of the Shuar community 'Nankints attacked police officers and military who were patrolling the mining camp La Esperanza in Morona Santiago Province, killing one police officer and injuring five other police officers and two servicemen. The Shuar attack followed months of militarization of canton San Juan Bosco and police and military forcibly evicting the indigenous community from their ancestral territory to facilitate the establishment of Chinese company Explorcobres S.A. mining project. Human rights organizations and indigenous confederations stated that the government carried out the evictions without respecting the constitutional rights of indigenous communities, such as the right to consultation prior to the prospection, exploitation, and commercialization of nonrenewable resources located in their ancestral land.

Acts of Violence, Discrimination, and Other Abuses Based on Sexual Orientation and Gender Identity

The constitution includes the principle of nondiscrimination and the right to decide one's sexual orientation as a right. The law also prohibits hate crimes. Although the law prohibits discrimination based on sexual orientation, LGBTI persons continued to suffer discrimination from both public and private bodies, particularly in education, employment, and access to health care. LGBTI organizations reported that transgender persons suffered more discrimination because they were more visible. A study by the National Statistics Institute in 2013 on LGBTI persons' social inclusion and rights found that 66 percent of transgender individuals suffered violence in public spaces.

In December 2015 the National Assembly approved a law on identity and civil data that enables individuals above the age of 18 to choose if they want to include their sex or gender on their government-issued identity cards. On August 3, the regulation allowing individuals to select gender on their identity cards entered into force. During the year the Ecuadorian Federation of LGBTI Organizations and the CNE met to define actions that would protect transgender voters from discrimination during the February 2017 national elections

The government, led by the human rights ombudsman, was generally responsive to concerns raised by the LGBTI community. Nevertheless, LGBTI groups claimed police and prosecutors did not thoroughly investigate deaths of LGBTI individuals, including when there was suspicion that the killing was because of sexual orientation or gender identity. LGBTI activists reported that law enforcement agencies had only resolved approximately 30 percent of the murder cases they had presented to authorities during the year. According to Silueta X, a Guayaquil-based NGO, transgender women were particularly vulnerable to violence motivated by sexual orientation or gender identity. LGBTI advocates estimated only 33 percent of cases involving violence due to sexual orientation or gender identity were reported to police and only one-third of reported cases were processed through the legal system. They noted that authorities had started to recognize these crimes as hate crimes.

LGBTI persons continued to report that the government sometimes denied their right of equal access to formal education. LGBTI students, particularly in the transgender community, sometimes were discouraged from attending classes (particularly in higher education). A 2015 UNESCO report stated that 25 percent of LGBTI students had been excluded from school activities because of their sexual orientation, while 26 percent had suffered physical violence during their studies. In June a representative in the office of equal opportunities at the University of Cuenca reported to media that she received 15 complaints from LBGTI students who had suffered discrimination during the previous quarter. LGBTI students, particularly transgender individuals, were more susceptible to bullying in schools, but human rights activists argued that the Ministry of Education and school administrators were slow to respond to complaints. The LGBTI population involved in the commercial sex trade reported abusive situations, extortion, and mistreatment by security forces.

LGBTI organizations and the government continued to report that private treatment centers confined LGBTI persons against their will to "cure" or "dehomosexualize" them, although such treatment is illegal. The clinics reportedly used cruel treatments, including rape, in an attempt to change LGBTI persons' sexual orientation. According to a local LGBTI organization, law enforcement officials closed at least two such clinics in Guayaquil during the year.

HIV and AIDS Social Stigma

The constitution specifically prohibits discrimination directed at persons with HIV/AIDS. There was limited societal violence against such persons. NGOs reported, however, that individuals with HIV/AIDS complained that they experienced discrimination, including in equal employment opportunities and access to appropriate health care. Civil society organizations criticized a lack of coordination between the Ministry of Health, Ministry of Economic and Social Inclusion, and local government institutions. They noted that testing centers existed but estimated that only 10 percent of persons with HIV/AIDS had been tested.

Section 7. Worker Rights

a. Freedom of Association and the Right to Collective Bargaining

A labor justice law that went into effect in April 2015 introduced some reforms to worker rights. This law, with some exceptions, provides for the rights of workers to form and join trade unions of their choice, bargain collectively, and conduct legal strikes. The law prohibits the dismissal of union members from the moment a union notifies the labor inspector of its general assembly until the formation of its first executive board, the first legal steps in forming a union. Employers are not required to reinstate workers fired for union activity but are required to pay compensation and fines to such workers. According to the Ministry of Labor, there were 4,000 labor unions in 2013, 80 percent of them in the public sector.

Companies that dismiss employees attempting to form a union or that dismiss union members exercising their rights face a fine of one year's annual salary for each individual wrongfully let go. The process to register a union often takes weeks or longer and is complicated, inhibiting union registration. Individual workers still employed may take complaints against employers to the Labor Inspection Office. Individuals no longer employed may take their complaints to courts charged with protecting labor rights. Unions may also take complaints to a tripartite arbitration board established to hear these complaints. These procedures often were subject to lengthy delays and appeals.

All private employers with a union are required to negotiate collectively when the union so requests. The law requires a minimum of 30 workers for the creation of an association, work committee, or labor union, and it does not allow foreign citizens to serve as trade union officers. The law prohibits employers from using domestic outsourcing, including subcontracting, third party, and hourly contracts, to avoid providing employees the right to form a union and to receive employee benefits.

The law provides for the right of private-sector employees to strike on their own behalf and conduct three-day solidarity strikes or boycotts on the behalf of other industries. The law also establishes, however, that all collective labor disputes be referred to courts of conciliation and arbitration. In 2014 the International Labor Organization (ILO) called on the government to amend this provision by limiting such compulsory arbitration to cases where both parties agree to arbitration and the strike involves the public servants who exercise authority in the name of the state or who perform essential services. As of November 1, the government had not taken any action.

In most industries the law requires a 10-day "cooling-off" period from the time a strike is declared before it can take effect. In the case of the agriculture and hospitality industries, where workers are needed for "permanent care," the law requires a 20-day "cooling-off" period from the day the strike is called, and workers cannot take possession of a workplace. During this time workers and employers must agree on how many workers are needed to ensure a minimum level of service, and at least 20 percent of the workforce must continue to work in order to provide essential services. The law provides that "the employer may contract substitute personnel" only when striking workers refuse to send the number of workers required to provide the minimum necessary services.

The law prohibits formation of unions and restricts the right to collective bargaining and striking of public-sector workers in "strategic sectors." Such sectors include workers in the health, environmental sanitation, education, justice, firefighting, social security, electrical energy, drinking water and sewage, hydrocarbon production, fuel processing, transport and distribution, public transportation, and post and telecommunications sectors. Some of the sectors defined as strategic exceed the ILO standard for essential services. Workers in these sectors attempting to strike may face charges with penalties of between two and five years' imprisonment. All unions in the public sector fall under the Confederation of Public Servants. Although the vast majority of public-sector workers also maintained membership in labor sector associations, the law does not allow such associations to bargain collectively or strike. In December 2015 the National Assembly amended the constitution to specify that only the private sector could engage in collective bargaining.

Government efforts to enforce legal protections of freedom of association and the right to collective bargaining often were inadequate and inconsistent.

Employers did not always respect freedom of association and collective bargaining. Although independent, unions often had strong ties to political movements.

On August 18, the Ministry of Education issued a resolution to dissolve the Union Nacional de Educadores (UNE), the largest teachers union in the country. The dissolution process started after UNE participated in meetings with international human rights organizations. On July 21, the Ministry of Education notified UNE that the government began the process to dissolve the union based on Article 22 of Executive Decree 739. On August 9, UNE asked the Ministry of Education to nullify the dissolution process due to legal inconsistencies. After the Ministry of Education issued the dissolution resolution, the national police raided the offices of UNE in Quito and Guayaquil on August 29 and seized UNE computers as part of the dissolution process. The ILO publicly rejected UNE's dissolution in a letter to President Correa.

During the year labor organizations reported several cases of workers fired for union activities. Labor activists reported that the government prevented strikes by detaining organizers the day prior to the planned demonstrations. Labor organizations also reported that, although illegal, some companies used outsourcing or domestic contract labor to avoid hiring workers with the rights to organize, form unions, and bargain collectively.

On October 20, *El Universo* newspaper reported that European Parliament legislator Ignazio Corrao agreed to publicize among EU institutions a case of alleged labor rights violations registered in exporting companies Dole, Noboa, and Reybanpac. According to the Agricultural Union Association of Banana Farmers, the violations included not affiliating employees to social security, paying them below the minimum wage, and not paying them any utilities, among others. Corrao stated that the free trade agreement between Ecuador and the EU required Ecuadorian companies to comply with the same labor rights standards as the EU. On November 11, the government and the EU signed a trade deal granting Ecuador access to the EU's regional free trade agreement with Colombia and Peru. As of December 1, the European Parliament had not approved the deal.

b. Prohibition of Forced or Compulsory Labor

The law prohibits all forms of forced or compulsory labor. The law does not require the means of force, fraud, or coercion for forced labor and includes all labor exploitation, child labor, illegal adoption, servile marriage, and the sale of tissues, fluids, and genetic materials of living persons. Penalties under this article range from 13 to 16 years' imprisonment. The law penalizes forced labor and other forms of exploitative labor, including all labor of children younger than age 15. Penalties for forced or exploitative labor are 10 to 13 years' imprisonment.

Authorities reported an increase in 2015 of children being subjected to forced labor in criminal activity, such as drug trafficking and robbery. The government identified and assisted 117 potential child trafficking victims; at least 87 of them were labor exploitation victims. Authorities convicted 31 traffickers in 2015. Limited resources, limited presence in parts of the country, and inadequate victim services, hampered the effectiveness of police and prosecutors.

Reports of forced labor of children (see section 7.c.) and women persisted. Observers most frequently reported women as victims of forced prostitution and domestic servitude. On July 28, *El Comercio* newspaper reported that several young women were contacted through social media, kidnapped after school, and taken abroad after being drugged. In some regions local gangs were involved in sex trafficking. Indigenous and Afro-Ecuadorians, as well as Colombian refugees and migrants (see section 7.d.), were particularly vulnerable to human trafficking. Traffickers often recruited children from impoverished families under false promises of employment; these children were then forced to beg or to work as domestic servants, in sweatshops, or as street and commercial vendors within the country or in other South American countries. An illegal armed group reportedly attempted to recruit children along the northern border with Colombia. Women and children were exploited in forced labor and sex trafficking abroad, including in other South American countries, the United States, and Europe. The country is a destination for Colombian, Peruvian, Paraguayan, and Cuban women and girls exploited in sex trafficking, domestic servitude, and forced begging.

Some Colombian migrant workers were reportedly victims of labor exploitation (also see section 7.d.), at times amounting to forced labor, on palm oil plantations. Research conducted by NGO Verite found that Colombian palm workers were subject to forced labor conditions. They were deceived about working conditions on palm plantations, they received as little as one-sixth the amount originally promised to them, they were forced to work overtime without pay, in some cases their wages were withheld, and they received threats of physical violence.

Also see the Department of State's *Trafficking in Persons Report* at www.state.gov/j/tip/rls/tiprpt/.

c. Prohibition of Child Labor and Minimum Age for Employment

The law sets the minimum working age for minors at 15 for all types of labor and the maximum hours a minor may work at six hours per day, five days per week. The law requires employers of minors who have not completed elementary school to give them two additional hours off from work to complete studies. The law requires employers to pay minors the same wages received by adults for the same type of employment and prohibits minors under the age of 18 from working in "dangerous and unhealthy" conditions. A ministerial accord issued in June 2015 lists 27 economic activities that qualify as dangerous and unhealthy. Other illegal activities, including slavery, prostitution, pornography, and drug trafficking, are punishable. The law identifies work that is "likely to harm the health, safety, or morals of a child," including work in mines, garbage dumps, slaughterhouses, livestock, fishing, textiles, logging, and domestic service; and any work environment requiring exposure to toxic or dangerous substances, dust, dangerous machinery, or loud noises.

The law establishes penalties for violations of child labor laws, including fines and closure of the business. Fines for violations of child labor laws range from $50 to $300 for parents or guardians and $200 to $1,000 for employers hiring children younger than age 15. These penalties were not sufficient to deter violations. If an employer commits a second child labor violation, inspectors may close the business temporarily. The law authorizes labor inspectors to conduct inspections at workplaces including factories, workshops, workers' homes, and any other location when they consider it appropriate or when an employer or worker requests an inspection.

The Ministries of Labor and of Economic and Social Inclusion and the Minors' Tribunal enforce child labor laws.

The government continued the "Ecuador without Child Labor by 2015" program, aimed at eliminating the worst forms of child labor. The program involved multiyear campaigns specifically targeting child labor in landfills, slaughterhouses, the agriculture industry, and begging. The government enrolled children in school, while also providing their families with financial assistance. The program was also successful in removing many children from the streets, where they often worked as street vendors or beggars. In the agricultural sector, the government worked with an established public/private working group to explain and enforce labor rules and educate families about the negative effects of child labor.

According to statistics published in June 2015 by the Institute on Statistics and Census, between 2006 and 2014 the overall child labor rate dropped from just over 9 percent to less than 3 percent. More than 73 percent of child laborers up to the age of 14 worked in agriculture, while trade and manufacturing represented 12.2 percent and 5.5 percent, respectively, of the overall child labor rate.

Several labor organizations and NGOs reported that child labor in the formal-employment sectors continued to decline. According to these groups, it was rare in virtually all formal-sector industries due to an increased number of government inspections, improved enforcement of government regulations, and self-enforcement by the private sector. For example, in the past several years, banana producers working with the Ministry of Agriculture and unions on a plan to eliminate child labor formed committees to certify when plantations used no child labor. These certification procedures do not apply to informal-sector, family-run banana farms.

Child labor remained a problem in the informal sector. In rural areas, where 15.5 percent of children worked, children were most likely found working in family-owned farms or businesses, including banana and rose farms. For example, government officials estimated that between 8 to 10 percent of minors in the workforce worked on banana plantations, although labor organizations reported that children were largely removed from the most heavy and dangerous work. Additionally, there were reports of rural children working in small-scale, family-run brick-making and gold-mining operations. In urban areas many children under age 15 worked informally to support themselves or to augment family income by street peddling, shining shoes, or begging.

Also see the Department of Labor's *Findings on the Worst Forms of Child Labor* at www.dol.gov/ilab/reports/child-labor/findings/.

d. Discrimination with Respect to Employment and Occupation

The law and regulations prohibit discrimination regarding race, sex, gender, disability, language, sexual orientation, and/or gender identity, HIV-positive status or other communicable diseases, or social status. The law prohibits employers from using discriminatory criteria in hiring, discriminating against unions, and retaliating against striking workers and their leaders. The government did not effectively enforce those laws and regulations.

Employment discrimination against women was prevalent, particularly with respect to economic opportunities for older women and for those in the lower economic strata. In March 2015 the Inter-American Development Bank reported the average income of women was 14 percent lower than that of men, although other studies indicated that women represented 56 percent of the university population and worked an average of 17 hours more per week. The female underemployment rate was 59 percent, 7 percent higher than the national underemployment rate and 10 points more than male underemployment. Afro-Ecuadorians reported that employers often would not interview persons whose job applications carried Afro-Ecuadorian photographs. Indigenous and LGBTI individuals also experienced employment discrimination.

e. Acceptable Conditions of Work

The minimum monthly wage was $366. Additional benefits mandated by law correspond to 40 percent of this salary. The official poverty level was $84.65 per month, and official extreme poverty level was $47.70 per month. According to official statistics published in June, 23.7 percent of the population lived at or below the poverty level, and 8.6 percent lived at or below the extreme poverty level.

The law limits the standard work period to 40 hours a week, eight hours a day, with two consecutive days of rest per week. Miners are limited to six hours a day and may only work one additional hour a day with premium pay. Premium pay is 1.5 times the basic salary for work done from 6 a.m. to 12 p.m. Work done from 12 a.m. to 6 a.m. receives twice the basic salary, although workers whose standard shift is at night receive a premium of 25 percent instead. Premium pay also applies to work done on weekends and holidays. Overtime is limited to no more than four hours a day and a total of 12 hours a week. Mandatory overtime is prohibited. Workers are entitled to a continuous 15-day annual vacation, including weekends, plus one extra day per year after five years of service. Different regulations regarding schedule and vacations apply to live-in domestic workers. The law mandates prison terms for employers who do not comply with the requirement of registering domestic workers with the Social Security Administration. The law provides for the health and safety of workers and outlines health and safety standards, which are current and appropriate for the country's main industries. These regulations and standards were not applied in the informal sector, which employed more than 52 percent of the population.

In March the Organic Law for the Promotion of Youth Work, Exceptional Regulation to the Working Day, Severance, and Unemployment Insurance went into effect. The law provides that Social Security contributors who have lost their job can opt for withdrawing their individual severance funds or can use the government's unemployment insurance, which includes a monthly payment for five months' equivalent to between 50 and 70 percent of the contributor's monthly average salary over the 12 months prior to the contributor's dismissal.

Enforcement of labor laws is the responsibility of the Ministry of Labor and the Social Security Administration. The government's 134 inspectors enforced all labor laws, including those for child labor.

Authorities may conduct labor inspections by appointment or after a worker complaint. If a worker requests an inspection and a Ministry of Labor inspector confirms a workplace hazard, the inspector then may close the workplace. Labor inspections generally occurred because of complaints, not as a preventive measure, and inspectors could not make unannounced visits. In some cases violations were remedied, but other cases were subjected to legal challenges that delayed changes for months. Penalties were limited to monetary fines between $950 and $6,360; they were not sufficient to deter violations and were often not enforced.

The Ministry of Labor continued its labor rights enforcement reforms by increasing labor inspections and increasing the number of workers protected by contracts, minimum wage standards, and registration for social security benefits. Various NGOs charged that the government rarely investigated complaints by migrants and refugees.

Most workers worked in the large informal sector and in rural areas. They were not subject to the minimum wage laws or legally mandated benefits. Occupational health and safety problems were more prevalent in the large informal sector. The law singles out the health and safety of miners, but the government did not enforce safety rules in informal small-scale mines, which made up the vast majority of enterprises in the mining sector. Migrants and refugees were particularly vulnerable to hazardous and exploitative working conditions.

Reports of abuses and insufficient government oversight continued in the palm oil industry, where many workers were Colombian refugees, other migrants, and fugitives from the law. The abuses included excessive work hours, very low or no wages, and inhuman living conditions.

Workers in the formal sector could generally remove themselves from situations that endangered health or safety without jeopardy to their employment, and authorities effectively protected employees in this situation. Workers in the informal sector received far fewer labor protections, and they were less likely to be able to remove themselves from dangerous health or safety situations without jeopardy to their employment.